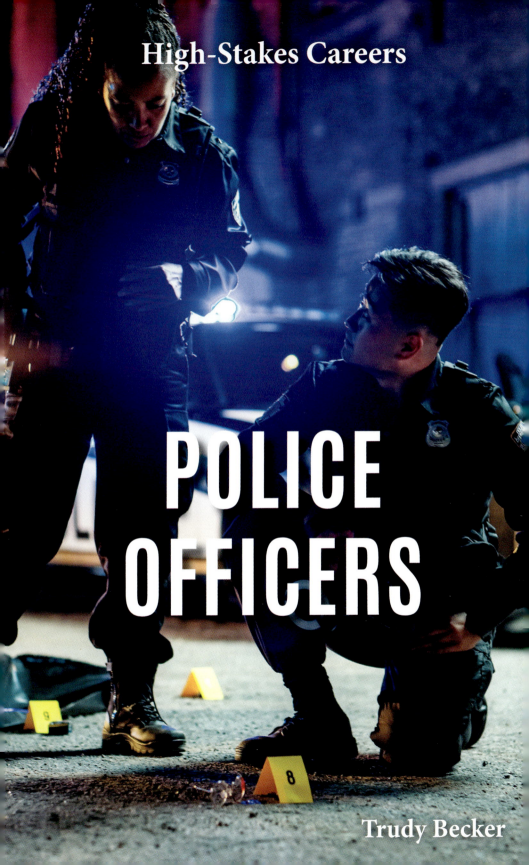

WWW.APEXEDITIONS.COM

Copyright © 2026 by Apex Editions, Mendota Heights, MN 55120. All rights reserved. No part of this book may be reproduced or utilized in any form or by any means without written permission from the publisher.

Apex is distributed by North Star Editions:
sales@northstareditions.com | 888-417-0195

Produced for Apex by Red Line Editorial.

Photographs ©: Shutterstock Images, cover, 1, 10–11, 12–13, 14–15, 16–17, 18–19, 20–21, 22–23, 24–25, 30–31, 32–33, 34–35, 36–37, 38–39, 40–41, 42–43, 44–45, 46–47, 50–51, 52–53, 56–57; Jim Rogash/Getty Images News/Getty, 4–5; Darren McCollester/Getty Images News/Getty Images, 6–7; iStockphoto, 8–9, 26–27, 58; Carolyn Kaster/AP Images, 29; Stephen Zenner/AFP/Getty Images, 49; Jeff Schrier/The Saginaw News/AP Images, 54–55

Library of Congress Control Number: 2025930923

ISBN
979-8-89250-672-4 (hardcover)
979-8-89250-706-6 (ebook pdf)
979-8-89250-690-8 (hosted ebook)

Printed in the United States of America
Mankato, MN
082025

NOTE TO PARENTS AND EDUCATORS

Apex books are designed to build literacy skills in striving readers. Exciting, high-interest content attracts and holds readers' attention. The text is carefully leveled to allow students to achieve success quickly.

TABLE OF CONTENTS

Chapter 1
CATCHING BOMBERS 4

Chapter 2
PATROL AND RESPOND 8

Chapter 3
FIGHTING CRIME 18

Story Spotlight
SECRET SERVICE 28

Chapter 4
COLLECTING EVIDENCE 31

Chapter 5
RISKS AND CHALLENGES 40

Story Spotlight
A DEADLY SHOT 48

Chapter 6
TRAINING 51

SKILLS CHECKLIST • 59
COMPREHENSION QUESTIONS • 60
GLOSSARY • 62
TO LEARN MORE • 63
ABOUT THE AUTHOR • 63
INDEX • 64

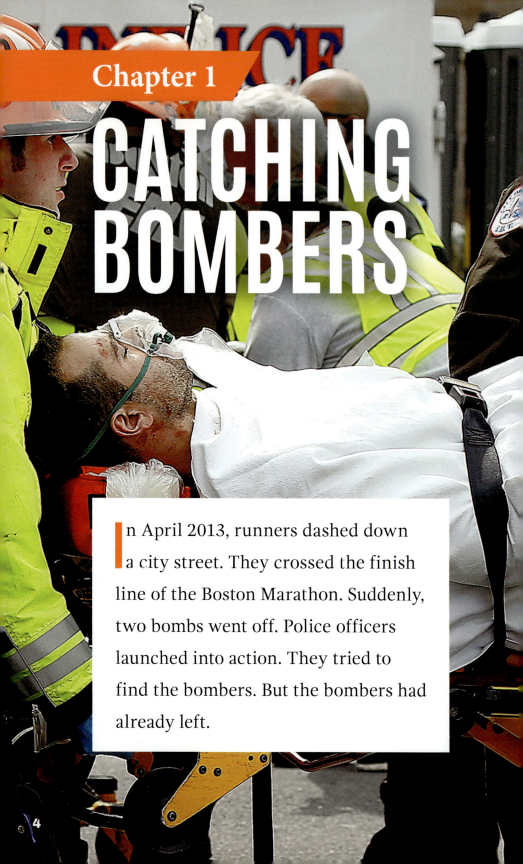

Chapter 1
CATCHING BOMBERS

In April 2013, runners dashed down a city street. They crossed the finish line of the Boston Marathon. Suddenly, two bombs went off. Police officers launched into action. They tried to find the bombers. But the bombers had already left.

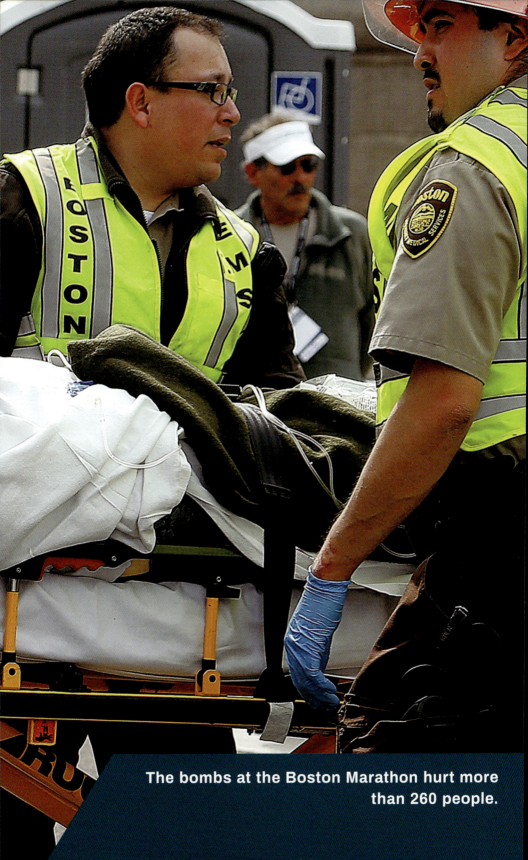

The bombs at the Boston Marathon hurt more than 260 people.

Police traced the bombers to the city of Watertown, Massachusetts.

The police started an investigation. After a few days, they learned who the bombers were. By then, the bombers had shot a police officer and stolen a car. The police found the bombers, and a fight broke out. Guns and bombs blazed. One bomber died. The other got away. Later, the police caught him.

TECH TOOLS

Security cameras helped the police identify the bombers. Officers watched videos of the marathon. The car that the bombers stole had a tracking system. So, police could see its location.

Chapter 2
PATROL AND RESPOND

Police officers work to enforce laws and keep people safe. Many officers go on patrol. They walk or drive through an area and watch for problems.

Some police officers patrol in pairs. Others travel alone.

Patrolling officers often watch for people who break traffic laws. For example, people may speed. Or drivers may not stop for red lights.

If officers see a dangerous driver, they turn their car's lights and sirens on. This tells the driver to pull over. If the driver broke a law, officers may give them a ticket. Officers also check if the driver is drunk or high.

Police in the United States make more than 50,000 traffic stops per day.

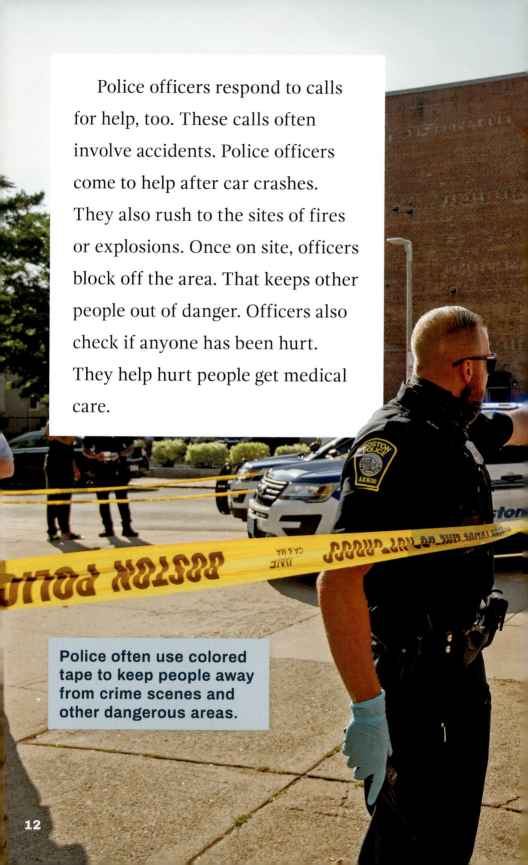

Police officers respond to calls for help, too. These calls often involve accidents. Police officers come to help after car crashes. They also rush to the sites of fires or explosions. Once on site, officers block off the area. That keeps other people out of danger. Officers also check if anyone has been hurt. They help hurt people get medical care.

Police often use colored tape to keep people away from crime scenes and other dangerous areas.

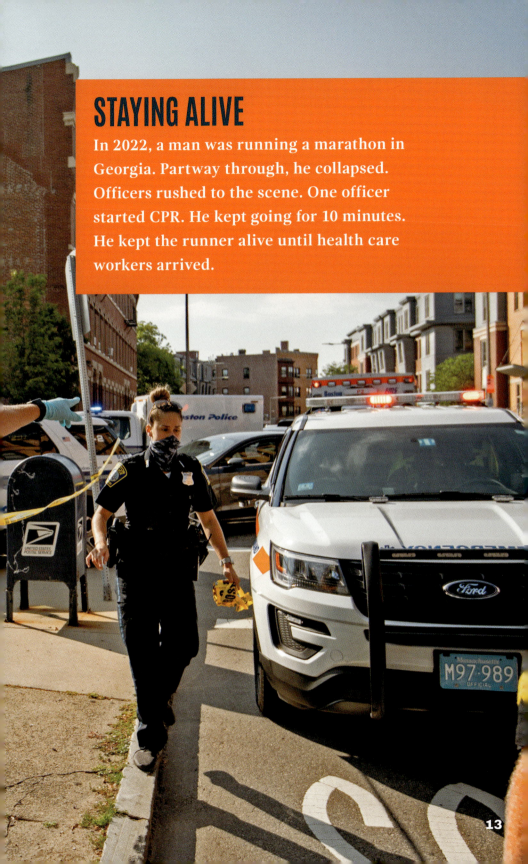

STAYING ALIVE

In 2022, a man was running a marathon in Georgia. Partway through, he collapsed. Officers rushed to the scene. One officer started CPR. He kept going for 10 minutes. He kept the runner alive until health care workers arrived.

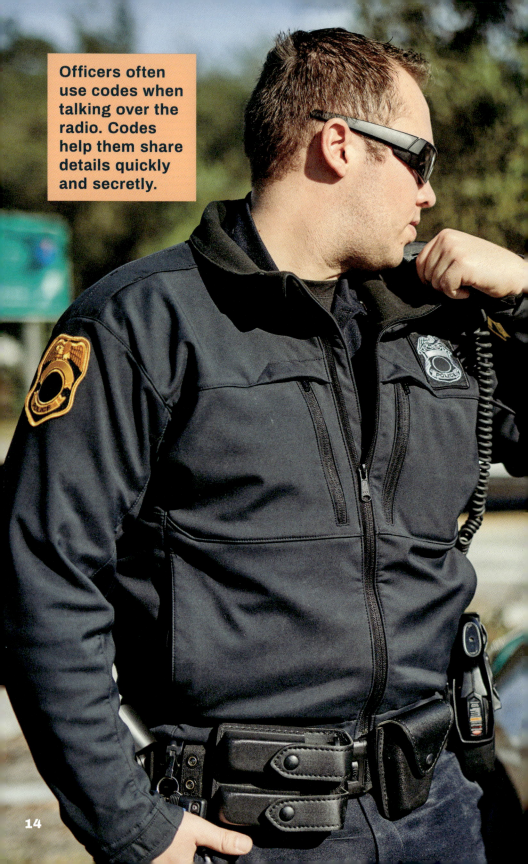

Officers often use codes when talking over the radio. Codes help them share details quickly and secretly.

Officers talk to one another as they work. They often use radios. Officers tell one another about accidents or crimes. They may also call for backup. Nearby officers rush to the scene to help.

WRITE IT DOWN

Officers write reports after every incident. Each report describes what happened, when, and where. It lists the people involved. And it tells what the officers did and saw. Reports help other officers understand what happened and plan what to do next.

Police officers may also act as guards. They watch over buildings or events. Some officers stand by the entrance. They check people going in and out. They aim to stop dangerous people from entering. Other officers direct traffic. They help people stay safe and orderly.

SECURITY STOP

In January 2025, a man in Washington, DC, carried several knives in a bag. He tried to enter the US Capitol Visitor Center. But police officers were guarding the entrance. They spotted the man's knives on their X-ray machine. They arrested him.

Traffic police often wear bright vests so that drivers can easily see them.

Chapter 3
FIGHTING CRIME

Sometimes, police officers stop crimes that are still in progress. Shoplifting is a common example. When thieves take things from stores, officers can help catch them.

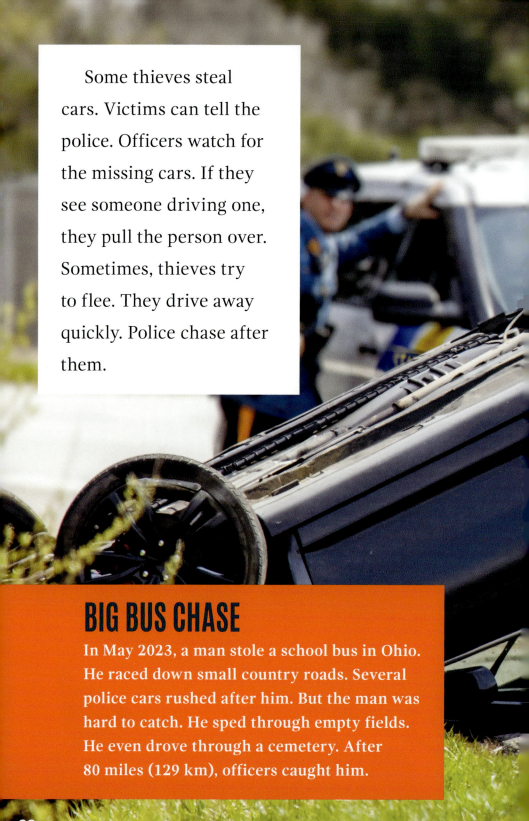

Some thieves steal cars. Victims can tell the police. Officers watch for the missing cars. If they see someone driving one, they pull the person over. Sometimes, thieves try to flee. They drive away quickly. Police chase after them.

BIG BUS CHASE

In May 2023, a man stole a school bus in Ohio. He raced down small country roads. Several police cars rushed after him. But the man was hard to catch. He sped through empty fields. He even drove through a cemetery. After 80 miles (129 km), officers caught him.

Car chases are dangerous. Some end in crashes.

For many calls, police try to stop violence. They may break up fights. Or they may respond to calls about domestic violence. That's when a person hurts someone in their household. Police go to the home. First, they stay outside and listen. If they hear shouting or other signs of danger, they may go inside. Officers work to calm people down. They try to keep people from hurting themselves or others.

Officers often knock or call out "Police!" before entering people's homes.

23

Officers get many calls about people with guns. If someone seems likely to shoot others, officers rush to the scene. They try to stop the shooter. Sometimes, officers can convince the shooter to put the gun down. Other times, officers must use force.

STOPPING A SHOOTER

In September 2023, a man in northern Virginia planned a mass shooting. He wanted to attack a church. The man posted his plan on social media. Someone saw the post and called the police. When the man arrived at the church, officers arrested him.

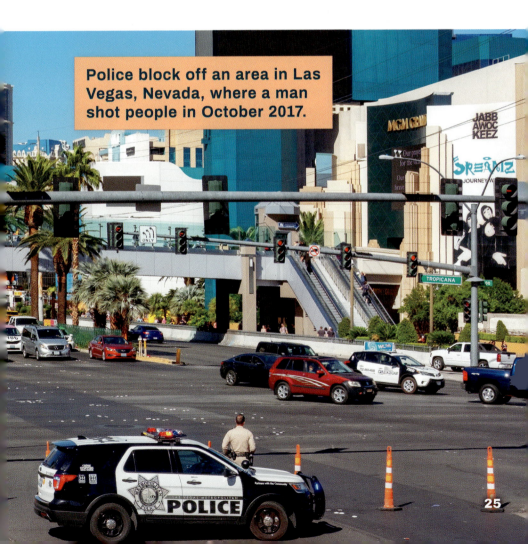

Police block off an area in Las Vegas, Nevada, where a man shot people in October 2017.

People on bomb squads wear thick suits. The suits help protect them if bombs explode.

26

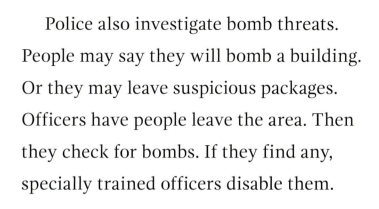

Police also investigate bomb threats. People may say they will bomb a building. Or they may leave suspicious packages. Officers have people leave the area. Then they check for bombs. If they find any, specially trained officers disable them.

BOMB SQUADS

Some police departments include bomb squads. These officers get extra training. They learn ways to stop bombs from going off. Being close to bombs is dangerous. So, bomb squads often use robots. Or they place tools near the bombs, then step back. The tools shoot and break the bombs.

27

Story Spotlight

SECRET SERVICE

In September 2024, a man tried to shoot Donald Trump. Trump was running for president. He was playing golf. The shooter waited behind bushes on the golf course. But Secret Service agents were there, too. These police officers protect US political leaders.

One agent spotted the man's gun. It was aimed at the agent. So, the agent shot at the bushes. The man ran away.

A witness saw the man drive off in a black SUV. Later that day, officers found and arrested him.

The shooter sneaked into the Trump International Golf Club in West Palm Beach, Florida.

Officers use gloves when collecting evidence. That way, they won't add their own fingerprints.

Chapter 4
COLLECTING EVIDENCE

S ome police work takes place after crimes happen. Officers try to figure out who did the crime, how, and when. To do this, they collect evidence.

Officers take many pictures of each crime scene. They also look for things people may have left behind. Examples include blood, hair, and DNA.

Officers interview people, too. They speak to witnesses, victims, and people who live nearby. All this information helps officers form a list of suspects.

SNIFFING FOR CLUES
Police dogs help with some cases. These dogs often use their sense of smell. They may follow the trail of a missing person. Or they may search for weapons or drugs.

Officers often find and study the weapons used during a crime.

Sometimes, officers think a crime is happening, but they don't have proof. For example, officers may think someone is selling illegal drugs. In these cases, officers may go undercover. They hide who they are. They may pretend to be criminals. Or they ask suspects to buy or sell something illegal. In this way, they catch people breaking the law.

UNDERCOVER BUST

In November 2024, Florida police thought a man was selling illegal drugs. So, an officer went undercover. The officer contacted the man. He asked about buying drugs. The two arranged to meet. A team of officers arrested the seller.

Undercover officers often use disguises. They use hats, clothes, and hairstyles to help hide who they are.

35

Once officers have enough evidence, they can get warrants. There are a few types of warrants. Some allow officers to search homes or other buildings. They may let officers take items to keep as evidence. Other warrants let officers arrest suspects.

A judge must review and sign each warrant.

Officers bring arrested suspects to a police station. They ask questions. Officers try to learn more details about the crime. If officers feel sure a suspect is guilty, they charge the person with the crime. People charged with crimes must go to court. The court then decides if they are guilty or innocent.

LINEUPS

Officers want to make sure they arrest the right people. Police lineups are one way to check this. Police place several people in a row. One person is the suspect. Then officers bring in someone who saw the crime take place. They ask this witness to say if anyone in the lineup is the person who did it.

Police must have enough evidence to charge people with crimes. Otherwise, they must let suspects go.

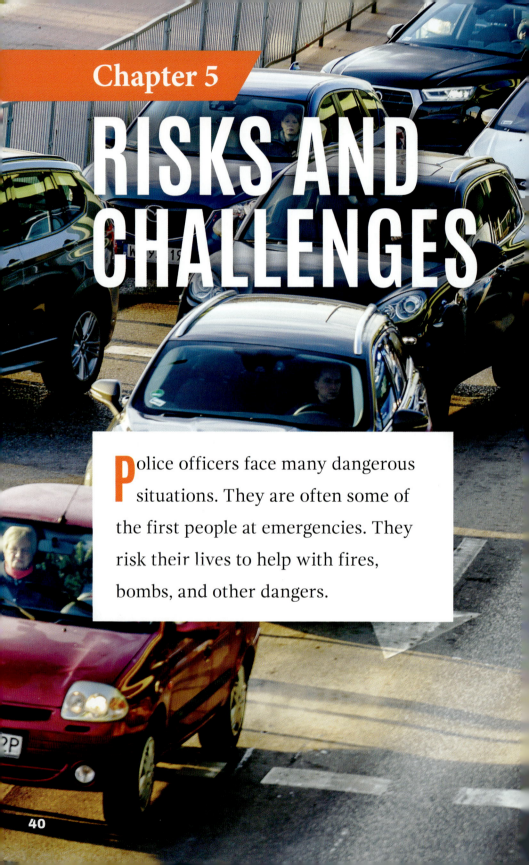

Chapter 5

RISKS AND CHALLENGES

Police officers face many dangerous situations. They are often some of the first people at emergencies. They risk their lives to help with fires, bombs, and other dangers.

Drivers often pull over so a police car can get through quickly.

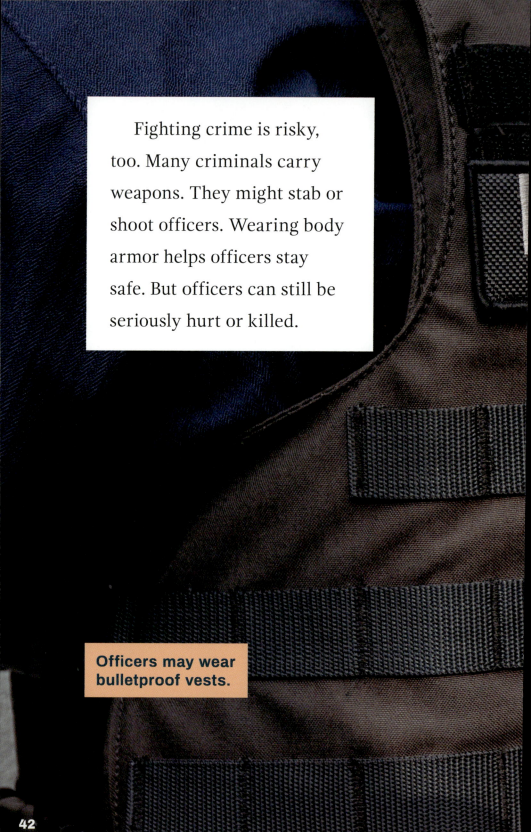

Fighting crime is risky, too. Many criminals carry weapons. They might stab or shoot officers. Wearing body armor helps officers stay safe. But officers can still be seriously hurt or killed.

Officers may wear bulletproof vests.

Officers may face attacks in other situations as well. They often work with people in high-stress situations. These people may be very upset. Police officers try to calm them down. But it doesn't always work. People may hurt themselves. Or they may lash out at officers.

BUILDING TRUST

Some communities don't trust the police. Officers may have arrested innocent people there in the past. Or they may have used lots of force. This history can make people uneasy. However, officers can work to gain trust. Police departments can hire people from the communities. And they can hold events to listen to people's worries.

At community events, officers can meet and talk with people. This helps both groups understand one another better.

Officers must think and act very quickly. They may have just a few seconds to choose how to respond to threats. That includes choosing whether to use force. For example, suppose an officer thinks a suspect is about to fire a gun. If the officer waits, the suspect could shoot them. But shooting is risky, too. If the officer is wrong, an innocent person could die.

In some cases, officers wear body cameras. The cameras record video. People can watch it afterward. This helps show what officers saw and did.

DEADLY FORCE DEBATE

In the 2020s, several cases of police using deadly force made headlines. They also sparked debate. Some people thought police should never use deadly force. Others said it was sometimes necessary. People spoke about biases, too. They pointed out that officers used force more often on people of color.

Police killed George Floyd while arresting him in May 2020. His death sparked protests across the United States.

47

Story Spotlight

A DEADLY SHOT

In December 2020, an Ohio officer saw a Black man named Andre Hill enter a house's garage. The officer thought Hill was stealing. He told Hill to come out. Hill did. He held a phone in his right hand. His left hand held keys. But the officer thought Hill had a gun. He shot Hill four times. Hill died.

The officer was arrested. After watching body camera video, a court found him guilty of murder.

People mourn the death of Andre Hill. He was shot by a police officer on December 22, 2020.

Some people get college degrees before becoming police officers. They often study laws and crimes.

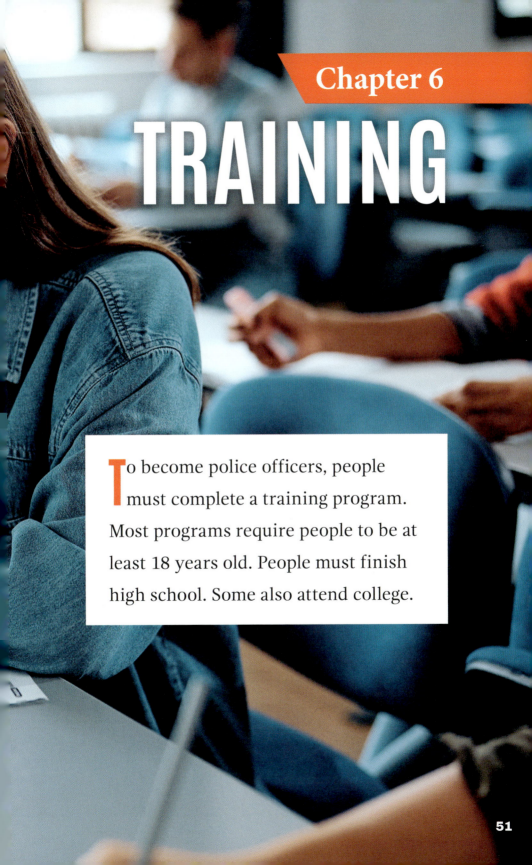

Chapter 6

TRAINING

To become police officers, people must complete a training program. Most programs require people to be at least 18 years old. People must finish high school. Some also attend college.

Officers use shooting ranges to practice their aim.

Training programs are sometimes called police academies. Most programs last a few months. Students learn how to respond to crimes and emergencies. They practice using guns safely. They also learn tips about communicating with people. Good communication can build trust and help officers keep people safe. Students must pass a written test about these topics. They must also pass fitness tests.

53

Field training is the next step. That's when new officers learn on the job. They pair up with experienced officers. Together, they patrol and respond to calls. The new officers practice using the skills they learned during training. After a few months, they are ready to work on their own.

YOUTH ACADEMIES

Some cities have youth police academies. In these programs, teenagers spend a few days learning about police work. They study topics such as gun safety and types of crimes. They may also get tours of police stations.

Some departments have programs that help high school students prepare for police jobs.

55

Some officers bring police dogs with them on patrol.

Some officers join special forces. For example, some become crisis negotiators. These officers speak with people in high-stress situations. These people often threaten to use violence. For example, they may take hostages. Negotiators try to get people to give up peacefully. They learn ways to calm and persuade people. Other officers join SWAT teams. They get extra training on ways to fight threats.

K-9 OFFICERS

K-9 units use police dogs. Each dog is paired with one officer, or handler. They work and train together. Training programs often last several weeks. The dogs learn many commands. Handlers learn to communicate with and care for their dogs.

✓ SKILLS CHECKLIST

- Being fast and strong
- Communicating well with others
- Knowing about laws and crimes
- Paying careful attention to details
- Thinking quickly under pressure
- Using weapons safely and carefully

COMPREHENSION QUESTIONS

Write your answers on a separate piece of paper.

1. Write a few sentences describing the training that police officers go through.

2. Which type of police work do you think is the most dangerous? Why?

3. What is one way that officers collect evidence?
   - A. taking pictures of crime scenes
   - B. writing speeding tickets
   - C. making arrests

4. In which situation might an officer work undercover?
   - A. when a person is caught robbing a bank
   - B. when a person is suspected of selling stolen items
   - C. when a person is arrested for stealing a car

5. What does **flee** mean in this book?

   *Sometimes, thieves try to **flee**. They drive away quickly.*

       A. escape
       B. stay still
       C. get caught

6. What does **experienced** mean in this book?

   *Field training is the next step. That's when new officers learn on the job. They pair up with **experienced** officers.*

       A. having no skill or practice
       B. having less skill or practice
       C. having more skill or practice

Answer key on page 64.

GLOSSARY

biases
Beliefs that cause people to treat others unequally, often based on what groups others are part of.

CPR
A treatment that can save a person whose heartbeat or breathing has stopped.

deadly force
Use of force that is likely to cause someone to die or be hurt very badly.

evidence
Clues that can be used to help solve crimes.

hostages
People held as prisoners so that someone's demands will be met.

incident
An event or accident that police respond to.

investigation
An attempt to find out the truth about something.

suspects
People the police think may be guilty of a crime.

suspicious
Seeming not right, not normal, or not allowed.

warrants
Orders from judges that allow officers to arrest people, search areas, or take things as evidence.

witness
A person who saw a crime happen.

TO LEARN MORE

BOOKS

Argentine, Cynthia. *Police Dogs.* Apex Editions, 2023.

Dolbear, Emily. *Police Officers on the Scene.* The Child's World, 2022.

Hamilton, John. *Patrol Cops.* Abdo Publishing, 2022.

ONLINE RESOURCES

Visit **www.apexeditions.com** to find links and resources related to this title.

ABOUT THE AUTHOR

Trudy Becker lives in Minneapolis, Minnesota. She likes exploring new places and loves anything involving books.

INDEX

accidents, 12, 15
arrests, 16, 25, 28, 34, 37–38, 45, 48

bombs, 4, 7, 27, 40
bomb squads, 27

calls, 12, 15, 22, 24–25, 54
cars, 7, 10, 12, 20
crimes, 15, 18, 31–32, 34, 38, 42, 53–54

dogs, 32, 57

emergencies, 40, 53
evidence, 31, 37

force, 24, 45–46

guns, 7, 24, 28, 46, 48, 53–54

investigating, 7, 27

laws, 8, 10, 34

patrolling, 8, 10, 54

radios, 15

special forces, 57
suspects, 32, 34, 37–38, 46

thieves, 18, 20
training, 27, 51, 53–54, 57

undercover, 34

victims, 20, 32
violence, 22, 57

warrants, 37
weapons, 32, 42
witnesses, 28, 32, 38

ANSWER KEY:
1. Answers will vary; 2. Answers will vary; 3. A; 4. B; 5. A; 6. C